Whatever you can

Vividly imagine,

Ardently desire,

Sincerely believe,

and Enthusiastically act on…

Must inevitably come to pass.

PAUL J. MEYER

Your
Success
GPS

Bud Bilanich
The Common Sense Guy

WALK THE TALK.COM

Resources for Personal and Professional Success

WALKTHETALK.COM

Resources for Personal and Professional Success

To order additional copies of this handbook,
or for information on other WALK THE TALK® products and services,
contact us at 1.888.822.9255 or visit www.walkthetalk.com

Your Success GPS

The WALK THE TALK Company
1100 Parker Square, Suite 250
Flower Mound, Texas 75028
972.899.8300

WALK THE TALK books may be purchased for educational, business or sales promotions use.

WALK THE TALK, The WALK THE TALK® Company, and WalkTheTalk.com® are registered trademarks of Performance Systems Corporation.

Printed in the United States of America.
10 9 8 7 6 5 4 3 2 1

ISBN-13: 978-1-885228-93-2
ISBN-10: 1-885228-93-7

Table of Contents

Your Success GPS

Your Success GPS

Have you ever had an idea come out of nowhere and whack you in the head so hard that you just had to act on it? I did. I got the idea for this book watching thousands of GPS ads during the recent holiday season. I was watching an ad one day and thought to myself, "Wouldn't it be cool if someone came up with a GPS for personal and professional success?" Then I thought, "Why not me? Why not now?"

The Global Positioning System (GPS) is a US space-based radionavigation system that provides reliable positioning, navigation, and timing services on a continuous worldwide basis. If you have a GPS receiver, the system will provide you with accurate location and information anywhere in the world.

Your Success GPS is an electronic and print-based success navigation system that provides reliable personal and professional success advice and a monitoring system to gauge your likelihood of achieving success.

The GPS is made up of three components: satellites orbiting the Earth; control and monitoring stations on Earth; and GPS receivers owned by individuals. If you have a GPS receiver you can accurately locate where you are and easily navigate to where you want to go.

Your Success GPS is also made up of three components: **commitment** to taking responsibility for your personal and professional success; **confidence** in your ability to succeed; and **competence** in a number of important success skills. It is available as an eBook and a printed book. With *Your Success GPS* system, you can determine where you are on the success arc and better navigate the twists and turns on your way to personal and professional success.

Disaster relief and emergency service organizations depend on the GPS for location and timing capability in their life-saving missions. You will come to rely on *Your Success GPS* to build the life and career you want.

How does *Your Success GPS* work? It's simple really. Think of each of the three components — your **commitment**, **confidence** and **competence** — as one side of a triangle. Now imagine a circle in the exact middle of that triangle. Your goal is to stay inside that circle.

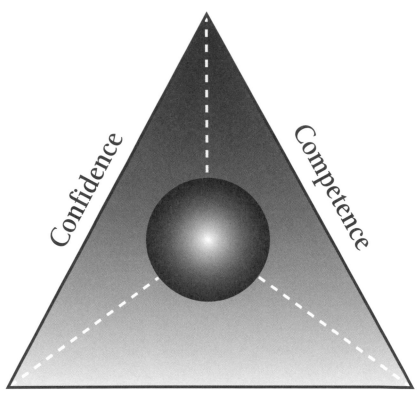

Occasionally, you will drift from that circle. You might experience some unexpected setbacks and look for someone or something to blame. You might have a temporary loss of confidence. You might forget what you know and make an error.

All of these things are normal and human. When they occur, do what you can to keep yourself inside the triangle, don't stray. Then make the course corrections that will bring you back to the center. If you remain in or around that circle, you'll be moving forward toward personal and professional success.

Taking off With Commitment

Taking off With Commitment

Have you ever noticed that the people who work the hardest seem to be the luckiest? Hard-working people take responsibility for their personal and professional success. If you want to succeed, you need to commit to taking responsibility and accountability for yourself and your success. It's that simple. You cannot succeed if you are not willing to take personal responsibility for your own success.

Personal responsibility is at the root of all personal and professional success. In *Straight Talk for Success,* I say...

> "It's simple, really. Success is all up to you, and me, and anyone else who wants it. We all have to take personal responsibility for our own success. I am the only one who can make me a success. You are the only one who can make you a success.
>
> "Personal responsibility means recognizing that you are responsible for your life and the choices you make. It means that you realize that while other people and events have an impact on your life, they don't have to shape your life. When you accept personal responsibility for your success, you own up to the fact that how you react to people and events is what's important. And you can choose how to react to every person you meet and everything that happens to you.

11

"The concept of personal responsibility is found in most writings on success. Stephen Covey's first of the seven habits of highly effective people is, 'Be proactive.' My friend John Miller's book *QBQ: the Question Behind the Question* asks readers to pose questions to themselves like, 'What can I do to become a top performer?' In his book and his speaking, John suggests that the key to success is taking personal responsibility for your life and career."

John is right. If you want to succeed, you need to commit to taking personal responsibility for your life and success.

Don't Ask Questions, Do the Job

Do you like inspirational books and cds? I do. Here's one that I like to share with people. *A Message to Garcia* is an inspirational essay written in 1899 by Elbert Hubbard. It celebrates the personal responsibility of a soldier named Andrew Summers Rowan who accomplished a daunting mission during the Spanish American War. As the American army prepared to invade Cuba which was then a Spanish colony, they wanted to contact Calixto Garcia e Iniguez, the leader of the Cuban insurgents to coordinate strategy. Rowan was chosen to deliver "a message to Garcia." He succeeded. In the essay, Mr. Hubbard points out that Rowan "asked no questions, made no objections, requested no help, and still accomplished his mission." He suggests that we should all take Rowan's example to heart and apply his diligence and sense of responsibility to our own lives.

A Message to Garcia was reprinted as a pamphlet and a book, selling over 40 million copies. Two movies were based on it. School children used to memorize the essay. It was very influential in American thinking until the middle of the 20th century.

If you would like to read the complete text of *A Message to Garcia,* go to http://www.BudBilanich.com/Garcia.

Ask, Believe, Work Hard, Receive

Have you read *The Secret* or seen the video? It is one of the world's best-selling books and videos. It outlines the law of attraction: Ask, Believe, Receive. While I believe that we attract what we put out into the universe, I also worry that people who take *The Secret* at face value may be doing themselves a disservice.

"Ask, Believe, Receive" sounds great. However, I think something is missing. My personal law of attraction works like this: "Ask, Believe, *Work Your Butt Off*, Receive." I have a framed quote from Paul J. Meyer hanging in my office. It reflects my view of the law of attraction and personal responsibility. "Whatever you can vividly imagine, ardently desire, sincerely believe and enthusiastically act on, must inevitably come to pass."

There's no two ways about it. Whether you prefer to think of it as "working your butt off" or "enthusiastically acting," the point is clear. You have to take personal responsibility for your success. I have to take personal responsibility for mine.

My books are a big part of my success. Many people ask me where I find the time to write my books. I don't find time, I just use what's available. I'm writing this on a Sunday. I'm on an airplane. The people around me are sleeping, reading, watching videos, listening to their iPods. I'm writing. I'm writing because airplane time is available time for me to think and write. Most of my books have been written on airplanes.

Judith Glaser is a friend of mine. In 2005, her book *Creating We* was named by *Forbes Magazine* as one of the 40 best business books of the year. Judith has a very busy consulting and coaching schedule. When I asked her where she found the time to write a 300+ page book while maintaining a busy consulting and speaking schedule, she told me that she got up at 4:00 in the morning five days a week and wrote for three hours for three years. She took personal responsibility for using the time available to her to create a business best seller.

The common sense point to all of this is simple. People whose Success GPS is working properly commit to taking personal responsibility for doing whatever it takes to succeed. They do the hard work necessary to achieve their dreams and their personal and professional success.

Stuff Happens: Choose to React Positively

Stuff happens: good stuff, bad stuff, frustrating stuff, unexpected stuff. Successful people respond to the stuff that happens in a positive way. Humans are the only animals with free will. That means we – you and me – get to decide how we react to every situation that comes up.

Have you ever had a major life crisis? I did. A little over 10 years ago, I found out that I had thyroid cancer – not a particularly deadly form of cancer, but cancer nonetheless. Trust me, you don't want to hear the words "you" and "cancer" in the same sentence. This experience qualified as some bad stuff.

It energized me. I remember thinking, "I've got a lot to do. I better get busy if I'm going to have surgery." I then got busy and rescheduled any client work that would conflict with the surgery.

I also learned everything I could about thyroid cancer. I talked to friends in the medical field who referred me to docs they knew who specialized in the disease. I went online and read, and read, and read. I interviewed a couple of surgeons and chose one to perform my surgery.

I visited a couple of online thyroid cancer support sites. I mostly didn't like what I found there – lots of angry people lashing out at one another, the unfairness of life in general and thyroid cancer in particular. I decided that if I were going to stay positive, it was best for me to stay away from the online cancer support groups.

In order to meet my client commitments, I had to spend the weekend before my surgery in New York. I finished up one engagement on a Friday and had to do a talk to some pharmaceutical execs on Monday. I had some downtime over the weekend, so I decided to visit a few museums and do some shopping. I bought a bright red striped tie that I wore to my talk on Monday. I still call it my cancer tie. I think it brings me luck. I wear it when I'm having a bad day.

After I finished the talk on Monday, the person running the program announced that this was going to be my last talk for a while as I was having cancer surgery the following Friday. People were incredulous. They asked, "What are you doing here when you're having cancer surgery in four days?"

I responded by saying that I had committed to doing this talk several months previous and that as long as I wasn't actually in the hospital I was going to do it – to the best of my knowledge thyroid cancer wasn't contagious.

The interesting thing about all of this was that I never considered canceling or postponing the talk. As long as I was able, I was going to honor my commitments. I chose to deal with cancer the way I choose to deal with most things in my life: honor my commitments, do the best I can.

My cancer story has a happy ending. I have been cancer-free ever since the operation and seem to be healthier than ever.

The one thing I was not going to do was wallow in anger and self-pity like so many of the people I met in the thyroid cancer online support groups. I chose life. I chose to be positive. I chose to honor my commitments to my clients as best I could. I spent a week at home recuperating. I conducted a week-long leadership seminar the following week.

The common sense point here has nothing to do with my cancer experience and everything to do with free will and personal responsibility. As you go through life, stuff will happen, most of it out of your control. The important thing is how you react to the stuff that happens to you — the nice things, the mild annoyances and the major catastrophes. It's your choice. Successful people choose to respond to events proactively. They do what they can to make the best out of any situation in which they find themselves.

I find a lot of wisdom in Native American spiritual traditions. The Navajos live in the arid plains of the US Southwest. Drought is always a problem for them. If you've ever been in Navajo country in New Mexico and Arizona you know what I mean. I once met a Navajo Medicine Man who summed up the difference between how white people and the Navajos deal with adverse situations. He said, "When there is no rain for a long time, the white man prays for rain. The Navajo prays to find the ability to live in harmony with the drought."

In other words, you have the ability to choose how you react to anything that happens to you. When *Your Success GPS* is functioning properly, you'll choose the proactive positive action, instead of the reactive negative one.

I have a friend who is a breast cancer survivor. She is a private person, so she asked me to not share her name in this case study. However, her story perfectly illustrates the idea of "Stuff Happens, But You Get to Choose What You'll Do."

After she was through with her cancer and reconstructive surgeries, she faced chemo treatments. Chemo treatments are extremely difficult, both physically and mentally. Most people retreat from the world as they undergo them — not my friend. Here is what she had to say in an email she sent me...

"I never quit work. I worked full time all through chemo and took time off only for the surgeries and various check-ups. I would have chemo on Friday, shot on Saturday, took to my bed Sunday and crawled to work Monday. By Tuesdays I was pretty good; second week better. And then we did it again. I'm sure you know how it goes.

"My nails are just growing back and my hair is still not long enough to give up the wig. My husband says otherwise, but he is a fan, not a critical style maven. He and my daughter were at every chemo. My daughter came home and spent the weekends with me. What a daughter. My husband was amazing as well. Guess hardship can bring out the best in people."

"Mid-November my daughter made us grandparents with a little girl. She has given us something to really put a smile on our faces."

Let this woman be a role model for you. Stuff does happen. But you do get to choose how you react to it. Remember, you're always in control of your actions. Be like my friend. Celebrate the fact that you have a loving, supportive family, rather than bemoaning the fact that you had breast cancer, reconstructive surgery and chemo treatments.

Navigating With Confidence

Navigating With Confidence

Self-confidence is the second of the three components of *Your Success GPS*. Successful people are self-confident people. If you want to become self-confident you need to do five things:

1. Become an optimist.

2. Face your fears and take action.

3. Surround yourself with positive people.

4. Find a mentor.

5. Become a mentor.

It's me who is my enemy

Me who beats me up

Me who makes the monsters

Me who strips my confidence.

— Paula Cole

Choose Optimism

By nature are you an optimist or a pessimist? I suggest you become an optimist. Learn from your mistakes then forget them. Use what you learn to help you do a better job next time.

Just like pessimism, optimism is a choice. It's up to you. Do you choose to see the glass as half empty or half full? I choose to see it as two thirds full.

I live by the Optimist Creed. I have promised myself "to be too large for worry, too noble for anger, too strong for fear, and too happy to permit the presence of trouble."

This is a tall order. Try as I do, I sometimes worry about things I can't control — like my elderly mother's declining health. I sometimes get angry about injustices in this world. I sometimes am afraid to take steps into the unknown — even though they have a lot of potential upside. I sometimes let trouble into my life.

As soon as I figure out that I'm letting worry, anger, fear and trouble into my life, I step back and look for a more positive alternative. I choose optimism.

A pessimist sees the difficulty in every opportunity;
an optimist sees the opportunity in every difficulty.

— Winston Churchill

The Optimist Creed

Promise yourself:

- To be so strong that nothing can disturb your peace of mind.

- To talk health, happiness and prosperity to every person you meet.

- To make all your friends feel that there is something worthwhile in them.

- To look at the sunny side of everything and make your optimism come true.

- To think only of the best, to work only for the best, and to expect only the best.

- To be just as enthusiastic about the success of others as you are your own.

- To forget the mistakes of the past and press on to the greater achievements of the future.

- To wear a cheerful countenance at all times and give a smile to every living creature you meet.

- To give so much time to the improvement of yourself that you have no time to criticize others.

- To be too large for worry, too noble for anger, too strong for fear, and too happy to permit the presence of trouble.

© Optimist International

Face Your Fears and Act

We're all afraid sometimes. I know I am. Aren't you? The secret to overcoming fear is to face it and take action. Action cures fear. Procrastination and inaction compound it. Failure is rarely fatal. Do something, anything that will move you closer to achieving your goals.

Fear will stop you in your tracks. Don't let it. When you find yourself procrastinating, you're probably afraid of something. Once you identify that fear you can begin taking some positive steps to deal with it.

Here are four simple, common sense steps for dealing with fear:

1. **Identify it.** Figure out why you're afraid. Once you've identified why you're afraid, you'll be well on your way to overcoming it.

2. **Admit it.** It's OK to be afraid. You wouldn't be human if you weren't afraid. Admitting your fear allows you to take the next step.

3. **Accept and embrace it.** Accepting and embracing your fear will give you the determination to do what it takes to move forward.

4. **Take action.** Action cures fear. You have to identify, admit to, and accept your fears first, but action is the most important of these four steps. Do something! The worst thing that can happen is that you'll find it was the wrong thing to do – and you will have eliminated at least one thing from your list of possible actions. Action is the antidote to fear.

Our greatest glory is not in never failing,

but in rising up every time we fail.

— Ralph Waldo Emerson

Surround Yourself With Positive People

What kind of people are in your life? Are they positive and upbeat, or are they negative? If you want to succeed, you need to surround yourself with positive people. Build a network of supportive friends. Jettison the negative people in your life. Pearl Buck is one of my favorite writers. In one of her books she says…

"There are many ways of breaking a heart. Stories are full of hearts broken by love, but what really breaks a heart is taking away its dream – whatever that dream might be."

Positive people help you realize your dreams. Negative people take them away. Positivity and optimism are contagious. Unfortunately, so are negativity and pessimism. Surround yourself with positive people, and you'll become positive and self-confident. On the other hand, surround yourself with negative people, and you'll become negative and lose your confidence. Self-confidence and negativity are mutually exclusive.

Negative people tend to come in two flavors: cynics and humorists. Cynics are not fun. They don't like much of anything. They're the kind of people who complain about having to pay taxes after winning the lottery. Humorists, on the other hand, can be seductive. They're clever and amusing. They go around with a smirk on their face, using humor to point out everything that's wrong. At first, they can be fun to be around. It's like the two of you have an inside joke on the world. In the long run though, their negativity will wear you out.

Set your boundaries. Walk away from the negative people you encounter. End your toxic friendships. It may be difficult at first, but as you move away from negative people, you'll become more positive and will attract positive people into your life.

23

And that is what is important — attracting positive people. Here are some of my best ideas on attracting positive people.

- **Think positively.** Train yourself to see the opportunity in every difficulty and the good in every person you meet. Be genuinely happy about not only your success — but the success of others in your life.

- **Smile.** Smiles are contagious. When you smile at others, they tend to return the favor. A smile can have a positive impact on someone who is having a bad day. By smiling, you'll attract other smiling positive people — the kind of people who will help you fulfill your dreams.

- **Speak positively.** You attract positive people when you say positive things. When someone greets me by saying, "How are you?" I always smile and answer, "Great, and you?" even if I'm having a tough day. This doesn't mean that I don't share my troubles with close friends. I just don't wear them on my sleeve.

A cynic not only reads bitter lessons from the past,

he is prematurely disappointed in the future.

— Sidney J. Harris

---

10 Powerful Phrases
For Positive People

If you want to become a positive person incorporate these ten phrases into your daily vocabulary...

1. You can do it.

2. I believe in you.

3. I'm proud of you.

4. Thank you.

5. I need you.

6. I trust you.

7. I respect you.

8. I appreciate you.

9. I value you.

10. I love you.

Find a Mentor to Help You

When you were young, I bet you looked to your parents and other adults for guidance and help in learning how to survive in the world. I know I did. We relied on these people to teach us what we needed to know to get through life.

Now, just like then, we need others to teach us what we need to know to achieve personal and professional success. These people are our mentors.

The term "mentor" comes from *The Odyssey*. Odysseus entrusted the care of his son, Telemachus, to Mentor when he set out to fight the Trojan War. The best mentors will help you learn and grow by sharing their knowledge and wisdom with you. In this way, you can benefit from their experience without having to suffer the consequences of gaining that experience firsthand.

Mentors are positive people by definition. It takes a positive person to give of himself or herself to help another learn, grow and succeed.

I have been fortunate to have had several mentors in my life and career. All of them shared several characteristics. They all...

- Were willing to share their wisdom, knowledge, skills and expertise.

- Had a positive outlook on life. They helped me through tough times and showed me how to find the opportunity in the difficulties I was facing.

- Were genuinely concerned about me and my success. In addition to being knowledgeable, they were empathetic.

- Really knew what they were doing. I respected them for their knowledge and skills.

- Kept growing themselves. All of my mentors were curious and inquisitive. Sometimes the roles were reversed. They asked what I was reading, and then read the books themselves — so they could learn and we could discuss the ideas.

- Gave me direct, constructive feedback. They held me to high standards. They congratulated me when I met their expectations. They corrected me when I failed to do so — but in a manner where I learned what not to do the next time.

- Were respected by their colleagues. Choosing someone who is highly regarded in his or her field or company is one of the best ways to identify a mentor.

- Sought out and valued the opinions of others. My best mentor always told me to listen most carefully to the people with whom I disagreed — in that way I might learn something. And, he was right.

Mentor: Someone whose hindsight

can become your foresight.

— Author Unknown

A Good Mentor...

 otivates you to accomplish more than you think you can.

 xpects the best from you.

 ever gives up on you or lets you give up on yourself.

 ells you the truth – even when it hurts.

 ccasionally kicks your butt.

 eally cares about you and your success.

Mentor Others

It's never too early to become a mentor. We all have something to give. The sooner you begin giving, the better. If you're in college, you can mentor high school students. If you're a recent graduate, you can mentor others still in school.

Mentoring is a great way to serve others. The more you serve others, the more confidence — and success — will come your way. Besides that, you'll find that you'll grow by mentoring. As you reflect on your life experiences and distill them into some nuggets that you can share with others, your knowledge will become wisdom.

Any mentoring relationship needs to focus on the person being mentored. While mentoring is most often a satisfying experience, remember that it's not about you — it's about the other person. Accept him or her for who he or she is. Help him or her proceed at his or her own pace. The best mentoring relationships are guided by the person being mentored.

Mentoring should be a positive experience for both parties. That means that you need to avoid treating a person you are mentoring as incompetent or incapable. Rather, think of him or her as someone lacking in experience who needs guidance. Don't criticize. Help the other person think through the consequences of his or her behavior and identify more positive ways of handling difficult or troubling situations.

Hold the person you are mentoring responsible for his or her success. Give him or her small assignments. Don't let him or her off the hook if he or she fails to complete them. Be willing to give of yourself and your time, but make sure the other person is doing so too.

Realize that the relationship will end. If you've done a good job, the person you are mentoring will need to move on at some point. It's all part of the cycle. It can be hard to let go, but feel good about seeing someone move on to bigger and better things — and another mentor.

Traveling on
Competence

Traveling on Competence

Create Positive Personal Impact

Do you know any people who have magnetic personalities? They are the people that everyone wants to be around, the people with whom everyone wants to work. These people know how to create positive personal impact. The ability to create positive personal impact is a fundamental competency for your success.

If you want to create positive personal impact, you need to do four things. 1) Develop, nurture and constantly promote your personal brand. Figure out the two or three things for which you want to be known. Consistently act in a manner that will get you known that way. 2) Dress for success; be impeccable in your presentation of self. Look in the mirror on your way out the door. Make sure that your appearance shows that you respect not only yourself, but the people you will meet that day. 3) Make sure your online presence is as powerful and polished as your personal appearance. People will Google you before they meet you in person. 4) Finally, know and follow the basic rules of etiquette. If you know the rules for a given social situation, you can concentrate on the conversation without having to worry about whether or not you are acting appropriately. Remember the most important etiquette rule of all is simple – make the people around you feel comfortable.

Build Your Brand

I'm sure you know who I mean when I say Oprah, Michael, Shaq, Tiger, Madonna and Bono. These are people who are powerful brands. However, personal brands aren't just for athletes and celebrities. All successful people create and nurture their own unique personal brand. Your brand is how others think of you. It is a combination of a lot of things — what you stand for, how you act, how you dress, your online presence. Nature abhors a vacuum. If you don't consciously create your brand, others will do it for you.

As you go about creating your personal brand, remember that a good brand will not appeal to everyone. A brand that appeals to everybody is too vanilla. You want a Cherry Garcia brand, something that is uniquely you. A good brand will appeal to a lot of people, but it will also turn off a certain portion of the population.

Take my Common Sense Guy brand. It appeals to a lot of people. However, some people find "common sense" a little too pedestrian and "guy" a little too colloquial. That's OK. Those folks probably aren't really interested in what I have to say and how I say it anyway.

There are two simple and common sense steps for creating a strong personal brand.

1. Decide how you want people to think of you.

2. Do whatever it takes to get them to think that way.

Stay on brand at all times. Be consistent and constant. Do whatever you can to reinforce your brand. For example, all of my websites have the words "common sense" in them. I end every one of my Success Common Sense blogs with a paragraph that begins, "The common sense point here is…" I avoid lengthy, complicated analyses. I work hard to simplify the complex and provide simple, easy-to-implement advice to my coaching clients. I use humor in my talks – and frequently pepper them with the words – "After all, it's just common sense, right?"

Once you decide on your personal brand, you need to take actions like this that reinforce it. Make sure your brand is clear, consistent and constant. Be on brand all the time in all that you do.

Be on brand in all that you do. People with strong personal brand ensure that everything they do and all that surrounds them, communicates their brand message.

— William Arruda

Dress for Success

Your appearance says a lot about you. Use it to enhance your personal and professional success. People do pay attention to how you look. That's why it's important to be impeccable in your presentation of self.

Dress one level up from what you have to. If jeans and T-shirts are acceptable attire at your workplace, wear khakis and a golf shirt. If khakis and golf shirts are acceptable, wear dress slacks or skirt and a tailored shirt or blouse. If ties aren't necessary, wear one every now and then. The common sense point here is that it's difficult to be overdressed.

Take care of your clothes and shoes. Make sure they are clean and pressed, and have all of their buttons. Keep your shoes shined and in good repair. Your belt should match your shoes. Wear tasteful, understated accessories.

Pause and look at yourself in the mirror on your way out the door in the morning. Ask yourself, "Does my appearance show that I respect myself and the people I'll meet today?" If yes, great. Go out and knock 'em dead. If no, go back and change into something more appropriate.

People judge us by the way we dress.

In all situations, business and social,

our outward appearance sends a message.

— Lydia Ramsey

Manage Your Online Presence

I used to think of being impeccable in your presentation of self as dressing well and looking good. But in today's world, you need to pay attention to not only how you dress, but what you post online and what other people post about you as well.

Check this out. A survey by CareerBuilder.com showed that 45% of employers use search engines and social-networking sites to research job candidates. If you don't buy this, think again. People do use search engines to learn about you before they meet you. Here's an example. Before she retired, Sylvia Montero was the Executive VP of HR for Pfizer Inc. She once told me that a woman who was booking her to speak at a conference said that she Googled her and was impressed by some of the things I said in a blog post about her.

Your web presence can enhance or detract from your image. Successful people use the web to enhance their brand and image. The first step is to see what's already out there about you on the web. Review at least the first five pages of results from search engines including Google, Yahoo and MSN. Then clean up your web image. Remove anything on MySpace or Facebook you wouldn't want your mother to see.

With ever smaller cameras and recording devices, it gets even more complicated. Now you have to pay attention to what others post about you online. I read an op-ed piece by a Harvard student who said that these days students worry about their friends posting pictures of them taken at parties. Apparently it's not uncommon for students with cell phone cameras to take photos of their friends engaged in inappropriate activities and shout "blackmail photo." Our public and private lives are becoming less distinct. A lot of what can get posted on the web about you is not in your control.

This doesn't mean you should have no fun, but it does mean you need to pay close attention to your behavior at all times. In some ways that's too bad. I know that I wouldn't want to have many of my college, or young adult, exploits posted on the web. Good thing for me that we didn't have cell phone cameras and web cams in those days.

Successful people create positive personal impact. If you want to create positive personal impact, you need to be impeccable in your presentation of self – in person and online. This means that you not only need to dress for success, you need to have a simple, easy-to-find clean web presence as well. It's really important to pay attention to your online presence as much as you do your personal appearance.

45% of employers use social-networking sites to research job candidates.

Be a Lady or Gentleman

If your mom was like mine, she always told you to be polite. And you know what? Our moms were right. You can never go wrong by acting like a lady or gentleman. Be mannerly and use proper etiquette. I try to act as a gentleman at all times. The words "lady" and "gentleman" may sound quaint and outdated to you. They're not. Successful people act like a lady or gentleman all the time. This gives them the polish they need to create positive personal impact and stand out from the crowd.

Manners are about kindness and caring about other people. Etiquette is protocol — rules of behavior that you need to learn and use. Manners come from your heart, etiquette comes from your head. Ladies and gentlemen are both well-mannered and follow the rules of etiquette.

If you know and follow the basic rules of etiquette, you won't look foolish in social situations. You will be admired for demonstrating class and confidence. Proper etiquette can help you get ahead in business because you will create a positive impression. Sometimes, you won't even know that people are watching.

Manners, on the other hand, distinguish you as a caring person, someone who values every human being. Well-mannered people treat every person they meet with a kindness that reinforces their self-worth. You can know and follow all the rules, but still not be well-mannered. While I think it's important to know and follow the rules, if I had to choose between manners and etiquette, manners would win every time.

The important thing is to be gracious. Do whatever you can to put other people at ease and to make them feel comfortable. Smile, offer to help in small ways, hold the door, initiate conversation. When you do these things, you will be creating positive personal impact. People will feel comfortable in your presence and will seek out your company.

For example, when you are dining with others, you may know that your water glass is on the right and that your bread and butter plate is on the left. Other people may not. If someone uses your bread plate, don't say "Hey, that's mine – yours is over there." Just place your roll on your dinner plate. Being right is no excuse for embarrassing someone else.

Ladies and gentlemen help people feel good

about themselves. They don't embarrass others.

— Bud Bilanich

Get It Done — Perform

As I'm sure you know, while good performance by itself will not guarantee your personal and professional success, it is an important key to success.

There are three things essential for becoming an outstanding performer. 1) You have to remain technically competent. The half life of knowledge gets shorter every day. Become a lifelong learner to remain technically competent throughout your career. 2) You need to set and achieve high goals. Set milestones to help you keep on track with your goals. Focus on your goals every day. Do at least one thing every day that moves you closer to accomplishing each of your goals. 3) You need to be well organized. Manage your time, stress, workspace and lifestyle well.

When performance exceeds ambition, the overlap is called success.

— Cullen Hightower

Become a Lifelong Learner

You probably have spent a lot of time in school. College, trade school, maybe graduate school too. You might be tempted to think that you needn't keep learning. After all, isn't learning what you need to know to function in the world of work the whole point of going to school? Not really. You just learn the basics in school.

Your education really begins when you start working. Thomas Carlyle once said, "What we become depends on what we read after all of the professors have finished with us. The greatest university of all is a collection of books."

Thomas Carlyle lived in the 19th century. If he were alive today, he might have amended his statement to say, "The Internet is the greatest university of all." It's true. So many of the great books, as well as other career and life success information, are available online. The important thing is to keep learning — how you do it and where you get your information is secondary.

I have a huge collection of books on a variety of subjects. These books are the first place I turn when I am looking for information to post on my blog, when I am working with my executive coaching clients, when I am preparing a speech and when I am designing a training program.

The half life of knowledge is getting shorter and shorter. If you don't keep learning, you won't even keep up; you'll fall behind in the knowledge that you need to become an outstanding performer.

As you've probably guessed, my best common sense suggestion for becoming a lifelong learner is simple. Read. Read technical journals. Read trade magazines. Read business publications like *The Wall Street Journal, Business Week, Fortune* and *Forbes*. If you think they're too stodgy, read *Fast Company*. Read your company's annual report. Read your competitors' annual reports. Read your local newspaper and *The New York Times*. Read news magazines like *Newsweek* and *Time*. Read business and industry blogs. Read books. Reading is the best way to stay up with what's happening in business, in your industry and in the world.

There are other things you can do to keep learning. Attend seminars. Join the major groups or trade associations for your industry. Attend their meetings and participate. Volunteer for committee work. Become known locally in your field. Take a class at your local university. Use your company's tuition reimbursement program to get a free undergraduate or graduate degree.

Your education doesn't stop when you graduate, it begins anew. There are many ways to keep learning. Decide which ones work for you, and then follow through. Outstanding performers are technically competent. They stay technically competent because they are lifelong learners.

Wisdom is not a product of schooling

but of the lifelong learning attempt to acquire it.

— Albert Einstein

Set and Achieve High Goals

Do you have personal and professional goals? Are they written? If you want to succeed, you need to set high goals for yourself – and then achieve them. Set goals that are S.M.A.R.T. (Specific, Measurable, Achievable, Results-Oriented and Time-Bound). Develop milestones for accomplishing your goals. Milestones are steps along the way to goal achievement. They keep you on track, and they motivate you by giving you reason to celebrate when you accomplish them.

All outstanding performers set goals. Then they meet or exceed them. They do this day after day, week after week, month after month, year after year. I am 58 years old, and have been in business for myself for 20 years. I set goals every year and develop quarterly milestones for those goals. I measure myself against these goals and milestones. It's a habit I developed when I was first out of college. It's served me well over the years.

Here are four tips for accomplishing your goals:

1. Write your goals. This makes it easier to commit to them.

2. Keep your goals with you so that you have a constant reminder of what you will accomplish.

3. Share your goals with the important people in your life. Goals become more real when you share them with others. And, others will hold you to them.

4. Focus on your goals several times a day. Ask yourself, "Is what I'm doing right now helping me achieve one of my goals?"

Never tell anyone that you're writing a book, going on a diet, exercising, taking a course, or quitting smoking. They'll encourage you to death.

— Lynn Johnston

Good Goals are S.M.A.R.T. Goals

 pecific

 easurable

 chievable

 esults-Oriented

 ime-Bound

Manage Yourself

If you're like me, I bet your life gets a little out of control occasionally. That's why it's important to get organized. Manage your life, your time and your stress well. Make sure that your life and worklife are in a balance that works for you. Occasionally, you'll probably find that your work-life balance is a little skewed towards work. That's OK. Just make sure that you work to get it back in balance as soon as you can.

If you're just beginning your career, you'll find that you'll need to spend more time at work — just so you get off on the right foot. Don't get overwhelmed by all of the demands on you. Most jobs are at least five days a week, eight hours a day, with work at home to keep up with projects and email. This is a lot different from college where you might have had a 9:00, 11:00 and 2:00 class, with the rest of the day available for reading and studying.

This increased level of demands on your time can lead to an unhealthy amount of stress in your life. Be proactive in dealing with this stress. Eat well and exercise. Don't party too much. If you find yourself getting too stressed, take 20 or 30 minutes and go for a walk to clear your head. One of my first mentors told me to H.A.L.T. By that, he meant don't get too Hungry, Angry, Lonely, or Tired. This is good advice for managing stress.

Put some order in your life. Develop a schedule and stick to it. Create an organizing system that works for you. Use your electronic gadgets to help you stay organized. Develop your own time-management system and work it. Focus on doing the few things important to achieving your goals, not the many trivial, but seemingly urgent things that will come your way every day.

Finally, don't procrastinate. Procrastination is a killer. It can hurt your self-confidence as well as your performance. Sometimes I procrastinate and find it difficult to begin big projects. They can seem overwhelming. That's why I always start big projects at the end of the day. That way, when I return to work in the morning, I feel as if I have some momentum going and the project doesn't seem as daunting.

Don't be fooled by the calendar.
There are only as many days in the year
as you make use of. One person gets only a week's value
out of a year while another person
gets a full year out of a week.

— Charles Richards

Communicate

Think about communication for a moment. I bet you spend a lot of your day speaking with others, writing emails and reports, or making presentations. All of these are communication activities. But are you doing a good job of communicating your thoughts and ideas?

There are three keys to dynamic communication: 1) You need to become an excellent conversationalist. Show a genuine interest in other people and what they have to say. Do what you can to help them reach their goals. 2) You need to write in a clear, concise, easily readable style. Write like you speak; imagine yourself in a conversation with the person reading your writing. 3) Finally, you need to present well – to groups of 2 or 200. All successful people have the ability to make dynamic presentations that move their audience to action.

The newest computer can merely compound, at speed,

the oldest problem in the relations between human beings,

and in the end the communicator will be confronted

with the age old problem of what to say and how to say it.

— Edward R. Murrow

Develop Your Conversation Skills

Have you ever watched a great conversationalist in action? Effective conversation, is an up-close and personal endeavor. All of the great communicators I know are great conversationalists. As with most things, I have one great piece of common sense advice on how to become a great conversationalist. Listen more than you speak. When I am in a conversation, I try to spend about one third of my time speaking and two thirds listening. I have found that this ratio works well for me.

Most people like to talk about themselves. The best way to get people speaking about themselves is to ask a lot of questions. When you meet people for the first time, ask what I call "get to know you" questions. You know the kind of questions I'm talking about here. "What do you do?" "Where do you live?" "Are you married?" "Do you have children?"

Listen to the answers and file away this information for future use. The other day I called on an old client. Prior to going to see him, I spent time thinking about what I knew about him from our previous conversations. Here's what I remembered. We know several people in common. His son is a music major at Ithaca College. His company was recently acquired.

I prepared for the conversation by coming up with four questions: 1) How is your son doing at Ithaca? 2) Have you spoken to Jo lately? 3) I saw Tom the other day, have you spoken to him recently? 4) How are things going with your new company?

By asking these questions, listening, and adding follow-up comments and/or questions, I was able to keep things moving for an hour. At the end of that time, I was in a good position to ask the two questions that were my main reason for the conversation. "How are things going with your team? How can I help you?" This was a sales call, after all.

The key here is to ask questions, listen to what people have to say and respond appropriately. Then file away what you've learned. I recommend writing it down so you won't forget. Review what you know about a person prior to visiting with him or her. This will help you prepare for the conversation by choosing the questions you want to ask.

44

Nature gave us one tongue and two ears

so we could hear twice as much as we speak.

— Epictetus

Write Clearly and Succinctly

Good writing will set you apart. Most people are poor writers. They are unclear. They ramble on. Their emails, letters and reports are a series of long sentences filled with big words that don't really say anything. You can catch people's attention by writing in a clear, crisp, concise manner.

I try to write like a journalist. I use short sentences with a simple subject-verb-object structure. My writing may read a little staccato-like, but it communicates. People can understand my points and the reasoning behind them.

Your objective in writing at work is to communicate — not to impress others with your vocabulary. When I was speaking with my niece about my book *Straight Talk for Success* at her graduation party, I said that I tried for an "avuncular hip" writing style. She said, "What does that mean?" I replied, "Avuncular means uncle-like. I wanted to sound like a hip uncle to people reading the book." She came back with a great question, "Why didn't you just say so?" She was right.

Write in short, simple sentences. Use the simplest words you can to get your point across, while still being accurate. Write fast. Get your thoughts on paper or the computer screen as quickly as you can. Then edit and rewrite until you've said exactly what you want to say. One of my first bosses always told me that rewriting is the secret to good writing.

Write with the reader in mind. Sometimes it's a good idea to read aloud what you've written to get a feel for how it will sound in your reader's mind.

My aim is to put down on paper what I see

and what I feel in the best and simplest way.

— Ernest Hemingway

Deliver Great Presentations

Finally, many a successful career has been built on one good presentation. Presentations give you an opportunity to shine. If you've ever benefited from a talk you gave, you know what I'm talking about.

Unfortunately many people are afraid of standing before an audience and telling their story. Their fear stops them from taking advantage of the opportunities presentations afford. Don't let this happen to you. Presenting is like any other process. It can be broken down into a series of manageable steps. Master the following five steps, and you'll become a great public speaker.

1. **Determine your message.** Begin by determining what you have to say. Get crystal clear on the message you have for the audience.

2. **Analyze your audience.** Why are they there? How much do they know about your topic? Are they familiar with any jargon you might use? What is their general attitude towards you and the information you will be communicating?

3. **Organize your information for impact.** I always start at the end. I write my closing first. I use this closing to help me choose the information I am going to include in my talk. I ask myself, "Does this information add to my main point?" If the answer is yes, I leave it in. If the answer is no, I take it out. Then I write my opening. I design my opening statements to do two things – get people's attention, and then tell them what I will be telling them in my talk. Once the closing and opening are written, I simply fill in the content.

4. **Create supporting visuals.** Once I've decided what I want to say, and how I want to say it, I develop my visuals. Your visuals should support your presentation — not drive it. There is nothing more boring than watching and listening to someone read his or her slides.

5. **Practice out loud.** This is the most important point of all. As an early mentor told me, "Bud, preparation makes up for a lack of talent." It also enhances your natural talent. Never skip this step. If you do, you will be likely to do a poor talk. And while a poor presentation generally is not a career killer, it is a missed opportunity.

It takes one hour of preparation for each minute

of presentation time.

— Wayne Burgraff

Be a Good Guy — or Gal

Interpersonal competence is the final key to success. 1) Become self-aware. Understand yourself and your impact on others. Use your self-awareness to better understand others and to increase your influence with them. 2) Build solid, long-lasting mutually beneficial relationships with other people. Strong relationships are a reliable indicator of interpersonal competence. Treat other people with dignity and respect, and they will reciprocate. 3) Finally, find ways to resolve conflicts with a minimal amount of problems and upset to relationships. Conflict is inevitable in business and life. Find ways to resolve conflict in a manner that enhances, not detracts from the relationships you've worked so hard to build.

Trust is the glue of life. It is the foundational principle that holds all relationships.

— Stephen R. Covey

Get to Know Yourself

Do you know any people who seem to have a deep sense of self-knowledge? These people tend to be interpersonally competent. They use their self-understanding to better understand others and to build and maintain long-term, mutually beneficial relationships with the important people in their lives. They resolve conflict in a positive manner.

You have to understand yourself if you want to understand others. Take a few minutes to answer the following questions:

- Do I like to spend time with people, or do I prefer to be by myself?

- Do I like to take in information in a structured step-by-step manner, or do I prefer getting a lot of information all at once and figuring out the connections for myself?

- Do I make decisions with my heart or with my head?

- Do I like to resolve things quickly, or do I like to wait until the last minute to commit to a course of action?

You probably lean to one or the other of the choices in the four questions above. Once you know this information, think about the people around you. How are they similar to you? How are they different?

For example, if you make decisions with your heart, you will have a difficult time convincing someone who makes decisions with his or her head to do something because "it is the right thing to do." Instead, you'll need to figure out the rational, logical reasons for what you want to do if you are going to convince a "head" person to go along with your ideas.

While it's important to know yourself, it's more important to know how you are similar to and different from others and how to use this knowledge to help you become more influential with them.

Knowing others is wisdom,

knowing yourself is enlightenment.

— Lao Tzu

Build Strong Relationships

Do you build relationships easily? Interpersonally competent people are good at building strong, lasting relationships. My best advice for relationship building is to "give with no expectation of anything in return." I know that it seems that the world works on quid pro quo. People expect it. That's why when you do something nice and unexpected for others and expect nothing in return, you'll be on your way to building strong relationships with them.

Here's an example. In a recent ezine, I featured a book by Valerie Sokolosky called *Do It Right*. I featured it because I thought it was a good book that would be beneficial to my readers. I also hoped that I would give Valerie some exposure to an audience she might not normally reach. The day after the newsletter went out I got this email from Valerie:

> *"Bud, you are so kind. I so appreciate this. And how can I help YOU????? This is what networking is all about. And coming from a place of abundance. You have my values, friend. Let me know how you are doing."*

Valerie and I are friends now — all because I took a little of my time to feature her book. My readers benefited, she benefited, and I benefited — all because I took a little step and did something with no expectation of anything in return. It's karmic really, it seems that very often you get things back when you least expect to.

Interpersonally competent people build relationships by doing for others. They don't keep score. They know that in the long run, good things will come back to them if they do good things for others.

Respect is the key to building strong relationships. In *Start Right, Stay Right* Steve Ventura offers some great advice on respect.

 ecognize the inherent worth of all human beings.

 liminate derogatory words and phrases from your vocabulary.

 peak with people – not at them, or about them.

 ractice empathy. Walk awhile in others' shoes.

 arn the respect of others through your behavior.

 onsider others' feelings before speaking or acting.

 reat everyone with dignity and courtesy.

Resolve Conflict Positively

If you're like most people, you occasionally find yourself in conflict – with friends, co-workers, your spouse or kids. Interpersonally competent people resolve conflict in a positive manner. No matter how interpersonally competent you are, or how easy-going you are, you will inevitably find yourself in conflict. People will not always agree with you, and you will not always agree with others.

My favorite method for dealing with conflict is counterintuitive. By definition, conflict is a state of disagreement. During a conflict, I focus on where we agree rather than where we don't.

I look for any small point of agreement and then try to build on it. I find that it is easier to reach a larger agreement when I build from a point of small agreement, rather than attempting to tear down the other person's points with which I don't agree.

Most people don't do this. They get caught up in proving their point. They hold on to it more strongly when someone else attacks it. If you turn around the discussion and say, "Let's focus on where we agree, and see if we can build something from there," you are making the situation less personal. Now the two of you are working together to figure out a mutually agreeable solution to your disagreement. You're not tearing down one another's arguments just to get your way. Try this. It works.

Try to find a WIN-WIN solution, in which both sides benefit.

In that way, conflicts are turned into opportunities.

— Robert Allen

Build Your R.A.T.E.ing

Certain words – nice, helpful, disagreeable, unpleasant – probably come to your mind when you think of the people you know. This is because, like most of us, you have placed the people in your life into mental categories of your own making. Have you ever stopped to think that other people are doing the same for you?

I have a model of customer service that I use with my consulting clients. It begins from the premise that after any interaction your customers R.A.T.E. you.

- **R** stands for Responsiveness;
- **A** stands for Assurance;
- **T** stands for Tangibles; and
- **E** stands for Empathy.

This model applies to interpersonal competence as well. The people in your life are constantly R.A.T.E.ing you too. You can use these R.A.T.E.ings to enhance your interpersonal competence.

If you notice, only one of the four points in the model – tangibles – is what you actually do for or deliver to the people in your life. You have to deliver the tangibles. You must produce results. That's the cost of a ticket to the success sweepstakes.

While tangibles are important, there are three other measures by which people judge you. They are focused not on what you do, but how you do it. They are emotional measures and are three times as important as the tangibles you deliver.

You have to pay attention to your levels of responsiveness, assurance, and empathy. Let's look at each of these three in detail.

Responsiveness. You have to ensure that the people in your life see you as someone who is willing to help, someone who understands what needs to be done and is willing to do it. You need to ensure that other people think of you as someone who will give them what they want, when they want it, and in a manner that they can use.

Assurance. You have to be able to convey trust and confidence. People need to feel that you are going to deliver. To do this, you must be very knowledgeable about the people in your life and their needs and wants. You need to be clear on what you can offer them to help them meet their goals. You need to ensure that they are confident that you will do what you say you will do.

Empathy. The people in your life must perceive you as an individual who understands, cares about, and pays attention to their needs. To do this, you need to be willing to walk a mile in others' shoes. You have to demonstrate to them that you are aware of, and sensitive to, their unique and individual needs.

Here's how you can improve your R.A.T.E.ing with the people in your life.

To improve your responsiveness:

- Every person is unique. Take the time to learn about every person you meet: his or her needs, issues and concerns.
- Listen to the people in your life. Make sure that they feel heard when they speak to you.

To improve your assurance:

- Make your word your bond.
- Stand behind you work.
- Admit your mistakes.
- Fix problems fast.

To improve your tangibles:

- Do what you say.
- Under-promise and over-deliver.

To improve your empathy:

- Listen – focus on understanding others.
- Empathize – put yourself in others' shoes.
- Acknowledge – show the other person you understand.
- Pamper – go the extra mile to help others.

Interpersonally competent people get high R.A.T.E.ings

from the people in their lives.

— Bud Bilanich

Get Positive R.A.T.E.ings

 Responsiveness
Your willingness to help others in a prompt and friendly manner

 Assurance
Your ability to convey trust, competence and confidence by doing what you say you'll do, dependably and accurately; a combination of knowledge and courtesy.

Tangibles
What you actually do for others.

 Empathy
The degree of caring and individualized attention you provide other people

Your Success GPS Snapshot

This little quiz is designed to give you valuable information on how well *Your Success GPS* is working. The first response that comes to mind is probably your best answer. Don't think too much, just respond honestly.

Yes No

[Y] [N] 1. I take personal responsibility for my own success. I understand that I cannot control what happens, but I can and do control how I react to what happens.

[Y] [N] 2. I am typically an optimistic person.

[Y] [N] 3. Fear rarely paralyzes me. I face my fears and take action.

[Y] [N] 4. I surround myself with positive people. In general, the people with whom I am the closest are positive and upbeat.

[Y] [N] 5. I have developed my unique personal brand.

[Y] [N] 6. I am on brand in all that I do.

[Y] [N] 7. I am impeccable in my presentation of self. I dress for success.

[Y] [N] 8. I understand and follow the basic rules of etiquette.

[Y] [N] 9. I am a lifelong learner. I actively pursue opportunities to learn and grow personally and professionally.

[Y] [N] 10. I have a well-defined set of goals for my personal development.

[Y] [N] 11. I have a well-defined set of business and/or work goals.

[Y] [N] 12. I manage my time well.

[Y] [N] 13. I manage my stress well.

[Y] [N] 14. My workspace is well organized.

[Y] [N] 15. I am physically fit.

[Y] [N] 16. I am a good conversationalist.

[Y] [N] 17. I write clearly and succinctly.

[Y] [N] 18. I am a strong presenter.

[Y] [N] 19. I understand myself and my motivations.

[Y] [N] 20. I use my self-awareness to help me understand others.

[Y] [N] 21. I am able to build strong, lasting, mutually beneficial relationships with the important people in my life.

[Y] [N] 22. I can resolve conflict with a minimal amount of disruption to my relationships.

Take a look at your answers. They provide a snapshot of how well *Your Success GPS* is working.

Highlight the statements for which you answered NO (there should be some…unless you're perfect). These are the areas you should work on in order to increase your personal and professional success. Develop action plans to address these areas. Make a personal commitment to see these plans through, and get started.

Congratulations for all those for which you checked YES. These are your strengths. Keep doing what you're doing!

Zero in on Your Destination and Get Going

Zero in on Your Destination and Get Going

Your Success GPS works only if you use it. If your car or mobile phone has GPS capability and you don't turn on the power, you get no benefit from it. The same is true with *Your Success GPS*. It works only if you use all three success components: commitment to taking personal responsibility for your success, self-confidence, and competence (and you keep them in balance).

I developed the Success GPS concept and wrote this book to provide you with useful information and knowledge on how to succeed in your life and career. But as the U.S. Steel pencils my dad brought home from work used to say, "Knowing is not enough."

When I was a kid, I was really fascinated and puzzled by these pencils. "Knowing is not enough — what the heck does that mean?" I used to think. I spent hours struggling with that idea. I was too stubborn to ask a grown-up.

I took a philosophy course my freshman year at Penn State in which we read Johann von Goethe. One day, as I was plowing through an assignment, I came across this quote: "Knowing is not enough; we must do. Willing is not enough; we must apply."

Boy, was I glad I took that course! It solved one of the profound mysteries of my childhood: "Knowing is not enough." In other words, you have to use what you learn, or what you learn isn't very valuable.

In this little book, I've worked hard to present my ideas on **commitment**, **confidence** and **competence** in a manner that provides you with simple, easy-to-use guidance on how to become a personal and professional success. It's up to you to think about what's here and decide if and how you are going to use it in a balanced manner.

If you're tracking with me, you realize that an overabundance of confidence and a lack of competence will not work. Similarly, the right mix of confidence and competence will not lead you to personal and professional success if you aren't willing to take personal responsibility.

As you go through life, you will encounter all types of roadblocks and setbacks. At times, you'll be tempted to whine, complain and blame — get over it. At other times, your confidence will be shaken to the core. Remember the Optimist Creed and "forget about the mistakes of the past and to press on to the greater achievements of the future." And at other times, your skills and expertise will let you down. When this happens, determine why you failed and what you need to learn to be better the next time.

The important thing is to stay focused and balanced. Commit to being responsible for your life and success. Remain confident in times of doubt. And keep your skills up to date.

Finally, I urge you not only to get going, but to keep going. As I often say in my talks, success is a journey, not a destination. As soon as you achieve one goal, you'll be likely to find several more on which you can set your sights.

Over 50 years ago, Abraham Maslow created his famous hierarchy of human needs. "Self-actualization" is at the top of the pyramid. Dr. Maslow, described self-actualization as "being all that you can be." He also said that self-actualization is an unobtainable state because as humans, we are hard wired to look above and beyond our present circumstances and accomplishments.

In other words, as soon as we think we've become all that we can be, we find that we can become more, someone better, someone who is capable of doing greater things and giving more back to this world.

That's why success truly is a journey and not a destination.

I wish you well on your journey. More importantly, I hope that you enjoy every single minute of it: the roadblocks, detours and setbacks as well as the victories, large and small, and the service you will be to others.

Here's one last quote. It comes from Teddy Roosevelt, 26th President of the United States.

It is not the critic who counts; nor the man who points out how the strong man stumbles, or where the doer of deeds could have done them better. The credit belongs to the man who is actually in the arena, whose face is marred by dust and sweat and blood; who strives valiantly; who errs, who comes up short again and again, because there is no effort without error and shortcoming; but who does actually strive to do the deeds; who knows great enthusiasms, the great devotions; who spends himself in a worthy cause; who at the best knows in the end the triumph of high achievement, and who at the worst, if he fails, at least fails while daring greatly, so that his place shall never be with those cold and timid souls who neither know victory nor defeat.

Promise yourself to live your life in the arena. Use *Your Success GPS* as a guide. **Get Committed. Get Confident. Get Competent. Succeed!**

The Author

Bud Bilanich
The Common Sense Guy

An internationally respected speaker, consultant, executive coach and author, Bud Bilanich is well-known for his business common sense. He brings a straight-forward, no-nonsense approach to his work of enhancing the performance of individuals, teams and organizations.

Bud received his doctorate from Harvard University, an M.B.A. from the University of Colorado and a B.S. from Penn State. Bud's common sense approach goes back to his roots in the steel country of Western Pennsylvania; he has over 30 years of experience in the organizational effectiveness field worldwide.

Bud is a sought-after, engaging and entertaining keynote speaker. Audiences worldwide have acclaimed his unique ability to simplify complex topics and present them in a down-to-earth, useful way. Bud is a cancer survivor and lives in Denver, Colorado, with his wife, Cathy. He is a retired rugby player, an avid cyclist and a film, live theater and crime fiction buff.

WALKTHETALK.COM

Resources for Personal and Professional Success

For over 30 years, WalkTheTalk.com has been dedicated to one simple goal… one single mission: *To provide you and your organization with high-impact resources for your personal and professional success.*

Walk The Talk Resources are designed to:

- Develop your skills and confidence
- Inspire your team
- Create customer enthusiasm
- Build leadership skills
- Stretch your mind
- Handle tough "people problems"
- Develop a culture of respect and responsibility
- And, most importantly, help you achieve your personal and professional goals

Contact the Walk The Talk team at
1.888.822.9255
or visit us at www.walkthetalk.com.

Other Books By Bud Bilanich
The Common Sense Guy

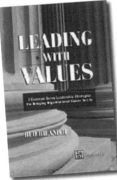

Leading with Values
Eight common sense leadership strategies
for bringing organizational values to life

$10.95

Solving Performance Problems...
A Leader's Toolkit
A common sense guide for leaders at all levels

$10.95

Straight Talk for Success
Common sense ideas that won't let you down

$19.95

Other Recommended Walk The Talk Resources

The Lead Right Library

14 Walk The Talk leadership "best sellers" on topics such as Coaching, Recognition, Ethics, Communication and much, much more. This powerful library is designed for leaders at all organizational levels.

$99.95

Serve Right Customer Service Learning Library

The perfect tool to help everyone in your organization deliver "best-in-class" customer service. The Serve Right Library includes 6 powerful customer service books.

$59.95

Dealing with Tough "People Problems" Library

6 high-impact handbooks designed to help leaders and managers at all levels deal with difficult "people problems."

$59.95

To order, please visit

WALKTHETALK.COM

Resources for Personal and Professional Success